FRENCH ARCHITECTURE